Original title:
Understory Chronicles

Copyright © 2025 Creative Arts Management OÜ
All rights reserved.

Author: Elliot Harrison
ISBN HARDBACK: 978-1-80567-262-3
ISBN PAPERBACK: 978-1-80567-561-7

Guardians of the Twilit Thicket

Squirrels in capes, they reign so high,
Defending their realm from pies flying by.
With acorn shields and branches for swords,
They battle the birds in their comic awards.

Raccoons in masks, they plot and they scheme,
Stealing the snacks in a nighttime dream.
With laughter and mischief, they dance in delight,
Guardians of silliness, stars of the night.

Beneath the Bark

Worms throw a party inside of a tree,
With music and laughter, so wild and free.
They dance in their tunnels, a wiggly show,
While ants serve up snacks, all in a row.

A centipede DJ spins records with flair,
While beetles all cheer, swiveling in air.
Beneath the bark, what a sight to behold,
With laughter and rhythm, their tales unfold.

Conversations with the Moss

Moss speaks in whispers, soft as a breeze,
Sharing the secrets of lives spent at ease.
It croaks about beetles who once wore a hat,
And laughed at a snail who was stuck on a mat.

They chuckle at shadows that stretch and they bend,
While lichen shares stories of where it all ends.
In the glades of the forest, under soft green,
Moss chats until twilight, such humor is seen.

Beneath the Twilight Canopy

Beneath the canopy, creatures collide,
Chasing their shadows while giggling wide.
Fireflies flicker, the lights in a race,
As raccoons exchange their best silly face.

Frogs croak a chorus, a ribbiting tune,
While owls spin tales about mischief and swoon.
In twilight's embrace, the laughter ignites,
Under the moon, where silliness bites.

Life in the Shade

In the shade, the squirrels chatter,
While mushrooms play a game of patter.
The sunlight dips, a sneaky guy,
While shadows dance and butterflies fly.

A raccoon runs with a grand old hat,
Winking gently at a sleeping cat.
The wise old owl lets out a hoot,
While ants march proud with their fruit loot.

Murmurs of the Sylvan Realm

The trees gossip in whispers low,
As chipmunks prance on a roly-poly show.
A fox in pajamas yawns with glee,
In a world of mischief, wild and free.

Frogs wear crowns made of sparkling dew,
While fireflies twinkle their nightly cue.
The wind tells tales of ages past,
As laughter among the branches casts.

Beneath the Giant's Veil

Beneath the giant's leafy cloak,
The mice sip tea and swap a joke.
A beetle plays a tiny tune,
While shadows sport beneath the moon.

With every rustle, secrets thrive,
As crickets dance and feel alive.
The laughter echoes through the grass,
In a world where troubles seldom pass.

Beneath Soft Ferns

Beneath soft ferns, the magic swirls,
As ladybugs wear their diamond pearls.
The shadows giggle, a playful lot,
With whispers of mischief from the spot.

A hedgehog rolls past, looking quite dapper,
Playing hide and seek, not one to taper.
The world is bright, despite the gloom,
In the heart of the forest, always room.

Hidden Wonders of the Wooded Realm

In the shade where the squirrels dance,
Mushrooms giggle, given a chance.
A raccoon wears a mask with pride,
Stealing snacks from each cabin inside.

A wise old owl gives quite the show,
With puns that only trees might know.
The ferns erupt in laughter, too,
As crickets chirp a silly tune anew.

Beneath the Branches of Time

The leaves whisper tales of old,
Where time is a story, not just bold.
A tortoise races with style and flair,
While the rabbits just giggle without a care.

A spider spins webs with comedic flair,
While ants practice dance without a care.
Moss throws a party, it's quite the ball,
But the trees stand guard, trying not to fall.

The Unseen Beat of the Forest

Beneath the rustling, there's music so sweet,
Where the loons and the frogs do their musical beat.
A beetle moonwalks with stylish charm,
While the buttercups giggle, causing alarm.

The wind joins in with a cheeky song,
As daisies sway, where they belong.
Nature's band, though slightly askew,
Makes every critter eager to pursue.

Secrets of the Green Tapestry

The dandelions plot with glee,
Hitching rides on a passing bee.
A chipmunk tells jokes no one can hear,
While the trees roll their eyes, full of cheer.

A brook tumbles over, laughing out loud,
While the mist dances lightly, oh so proud.
In this green stage, every creature's a star,
Crafting tales of whimsy, near and far.

Silence of the Subterranean Realm

In the dark where roots take naps,
Worms plot schemes, sharing laughs.
Mice in tuxedos dance around,
Echoes of joy, no sight or sound.

Raccoons wear masks, feeling sly,
Discussing secrets, oh me, oh my!
They gossip low, beneath the ground,
Each tale twisted, hilariously wound.

A beetle brags of his great race,
While ants march on, keeping pace.
"Look at me!" shrieks a toad in flair,
Hopping around in his fancy lair.

Beneath the dirt, where jokes run deep,
Laughter stirs, but all must sleep.
In this world of quirky scenes,
Nature's jesters thrive in green!

The Dance of the Forgotten Foliage

Leaves sway gently in a breeze,
Old trees giggle, if you please.
Whispers of laughter fill the air,
As ferns perform without a care.

Mushrooms don top hats, so bright,
Jigging under the pale moonlight.
"Who needs a ball?" a thistle exclaims,
"Just bring your friends, we'll play some games!"

Squirrels two-step, they twirl and spin,
While hedgehogs clap, their tiny kin.
Ribbons of ivy swirl and twine,
Dancing together, looking divine.

Nature's party; oh what a sight,
With every creature enjoying the night.
In the green ballroom, laughter's a must,
Where fun takes root, and peace is just.

Beneath Nature's Gentle Guard

Tiny critters in hats parade,
Under leaves, their shade is made.
A snail takes time, he's lost in thought,
Plotting adventures, but not a lot.

A mole can't see but hears the fun,
Singing along, just one by one.
The earth chuckles, a soft delight,
As shadows dance through day and night.

Grasshoppers leap to tell a tale,
Of silly mishaps on a snail's trail.
"Why rush?" chirps a cricket bright,
"When every moment's pure delight!"

In this realm where humor grows,
Nature's quirks nobody knows.
From burrows deep, they share their mirth,
Creating joy beneath the earth.

A Symphony of Subtle Colors

Petals whisper in hues so bright,
Dancing about in sheer delight.
A dandelion sings off-key,
"But who cares?" the bluebell agrees.

Butterflies giggle, twirling around,
With skirts of gold and a joyful sound.
Pollinators play hide and seek,
While blooms laugh out; it's fun they speak!

An old oak jests with a sway and spin,
"Join the party, come on, bring a grin!"
With roots in rhythm and leaves in tune,
Nature's ruckus beneath the moon.

In this concert, colors collide,
With laughter echoing far and wide.
The flora and fauna, hand in hand,
Composing joy in a vibrant land.

The Hidden Symphony with the Earth

In the soil, the worms do dance,
To a tune that leaves them in a trance.
They wiggle and jiggle with pure delight,
While ants form a band, oh what a sight!

Fungi in capes, taking the stage,
Mushrooms conducting, quite the rage.
Raccoons clapped paws, a wild ruckus,
As frogs croaked loud, making a fuss.

Beneath our feet, a realm galore,
Where beetles tap-dance and giggle some more.
Trees sway gently to a breezy beat,
While bees form a choir, buzzing so sweet!

Nature's jesters in an earthy show,
Wondrous melodies swaying to and fro.
A hidden symphony that never stops,
In this merry world, the laughter pops!

Chronicles of the Caretakers Below

The moles wear glasses, digging their way,
In their underground library, they read all day.
With tiny paws flipping pages with glee,
They giggle at stories of the big oak tree.

The gophers hold meetings, every week,
Complaining of fescue, it's not what they seek.
Nibbles and bites over cups of seeds,
They plot with mischief, as boredom leads!

In the burrows, the chatter never dies,
A gossip fest where no one is shy.
With secrets of roots and tattle-tale ferns,
Each tale giggles as the earthworm turns.

So here's to the caretakers hidden from sight,
With their funny adventures, they bring sheer delight.
In every crack and crevice, they play,
Making history where the brave hearts stray!

Shadows of the Forest Aflame

Under canopies, whispers arise,
Where shadows dance, oh what a surprise!
Squirrels joke as they leap through the air,
While shadows play tag without a care!

The owls chuckle, giving wise advice,
"Don't eat the berries, they're really quite nice!"
Raccoons argue over shiny things,
With giggles that bounce on the breeze as it sings.

Sunlight flickers in a patchwork array,
Creating a stage for the prancing jay.
"Did you see that worm? It's a real big one!"
They laugh as they tumble, just having some fun.

In this forest of shadows, all is bright,
With mischief and capers from morning to night.
Aflame with laughter, beneath the trees,
Nature's jesters dance on the gentle breeze!

Nature's Veiled Companions

In the ferns, the gnomes do reside,
With tiny hats and a knack to hide.
They giggle when travelers pass by,
Offering two cents and a cheeky sigh.

Butterflies flirt, with colors so bold,
Blushing as flowers give tales of old.
"Did you hear the news?" says a whispering breeze,
"A snail just won a race, oh what a tease!"

Bees in a rally, buzzing about,
Politely discussing the nectar route.
While squirrels just roll in the leaves with cheer,
Saying, "Who cares? It's all fun out here!"

Nature's companions, fun-filled and spry,
Veiling their secrets where mischief can lie.
In each little nook, they giggle and play,
In a world full of wonder, they brighten our day!

Glimpses of the Untold Canopy

Squirrels plotting up in the trees,
Chasing each other, oh, such a tease.
One's got a nut, while the other just stares,
Wondering why life leads to such dares.

A raccoon crafts plans late in the night,
Wearing a mask, he prepares for a bite.
Sneaking around, he thinks he's so slick,
But caught in the act, he's gone in a flick.

A chameleon plays hide-and-seek,
Changing his colors, so sly and so meek.
The frog on a leaf snickers with glee,
"I can't change my skin, but I still look like me!"

Woodpeckers tapping, making a beat,
Weird birdy disco, oh what a treat.
They dance through the branches, wild and free,
In the realm of the trees, it's a funny decree.

Beneath the Curtain of Foliage

Beneath the leaves, where shadows play,
Lies a snail trying to find his way.
He's got no rush, he's on a grand quest,
Running races? No, he's just taking a rest.

The ladybug laughs, counting her spots,
While a jittery ant takes up the slots.
"Who's faster?" they query, "Come place your bets!"
But with tiny feet, where's the fun in the stress?

A spider spins tales with silken delight,
While a moth brings popcorn to the night.
Creepy and crawly, they party with flair,
Making strange buddies and filling the air.

Then a bluebird tweets from high above,
Sharing old secrets with a dash of love.
In the thick of the green, hilarity thrives,
Amongst all the critters, oh how fun it arrives!

Spells of the Green Abyss

In a thicket, the toads play a game,
Croaking like opera stars, oh what a fame.
With each jumping round, they raise a cheer,
Celebrating each leap with a froggy leer.

Beneath the ferns, where shadows entrap,
A wise old turtle springs into a nap.
"Why rush through life?" he says with a grin,
As the world spins by with its usual din.

A wisecracking woodpecker calls out loud,
To a sarcastic crow perched near the cloud.
"Life's like a riddle, wrapped in a song,"
"Just don't get stuck where the beetles go wrong!"

With giggles of laughter all through the night,
The forest comes alive, it's pure delight.
In this green land, with joy they confess,
Life's not so serious, it's just a mess!

Illuminated by Nature's Secrets

A glowworm glimmers, lighting up paths,
While a witty owl cracks up with laughs.
"Who's up all night?" he hoots with a wink,
"Just me and my buddies, come have a drink!"

The hedgehogs gather to share old tales,
Of great adventures, and shipwrecked snails.
"Hitchhiking's tough when the road's so long,"
But they know laughter is where they belong.

The fireflies dance, a flickering spree,
Trying to impress a bemused bumblebee.
With winks and flashes, they light up the dusk,
In a world full of fun, no place for disgust.

So come join this party among trees and moss,
Where giggly gizmos unite without loss.
With nature's secrets bringing smile and cheer,
Every day's magic is vividly clear.

The Quiet Pulse of Nature

In the shade where critters dance,
A snail took a slide, missed his chance.
The squirrels chuckle in the trees,
As the owl snores on with such ease.

A sleepy frog croaks a tune,
While butterflies flirt with the moon.
The whispering leaves share a laugh,
At the raccoon stuck in a half.

The breeze tells tales of the night,
As fireflies flicker, oh what a sight!
Nature's pulse has a silly beat,
Where even roots tap their feet.

Underneath where shadows play,
The mushrooms giggle, come what may.
Nature's humor flows like a stream,
In this whimsical leafy dream.

Hushed Stories in the Glade

In the glade where ferns sway low,
A gossiping beetle steals the show.
The partridge gets lost on her way,
And the lazy ants all yell 'Hooray!'

A critter's picnic, a perfect spread,
Till the wind blows the sandwich ahead.
Soggy croutons fly like a missile,
Impacting the mole's snout with a whistle.

The toads take bets on a race,
While wildflowers giggle, keeping pace.
Bees barter honey for silly tales,
While the daisies bloom with little jails.

A time-out for all the sly foxes,
Laughing at the fate of old boxes.
Hushed stories in the leafy shade,
Fill the air with lighthearted trade.

Life Below the Canopy

Below the leaves, a party's begun,
With ants in tuxedos, oh what fun!
A grasshopper brings his ukulele,
While the glowworms dance, quite gaily.

A hedgehog rolls by with a grin,
Giving a piggyback ride to a bin.
The mushrooms argue, who's the best chef?
While dandelions puff and say, 'Beef!'

The comic fox juggles acorns,
As curious hedgehogs raise their horns.
Beneath it all, a wise old tree,
Says life's a jest, come laugh with me!

The chatter fades when the moon's in sight,
And tales are spun until it's daylight.
Life below, such a merry spree,
Nature's laughter, wild and free.

The Veiled Narrative of Roots

Beneath the soil, a tale unfolds,
Where tangled roots have secrets bold.
The glories of life, they like to share,
With whispers soft, floating in the air.

The mole's planning a burrowed prank,
But the gophers laugh, oh how they tank!
While the worms write scripts in the muck,
Plotting their plays on luck and pluck.

The roots exchange jokes, a merry bunch,
As the fungi feast on a lunch crunch.
The veil of dirt hides much intrigue,
With laughter echoing through each league.

When the rain comes, muddy affairs,
Mischief abounds in moist layers.
Roots laugh together, plot and tease,
In a world where joy's carried on the breeze.

Legends of the Lush Underbrush

In the thicket, a squirrel sneaks,
With acorns tucked and lofty peaks.
He's a pirate of the forest floor,
Claiming treasure, oh what a bore!

A hedgehog dons a tiny hat,
Sipping tea with a cheeky cat.
They laugh at leaves that twist and twirl,
As petals dance and daisies swirl.

The rabbits host a dance-off night,
With carrots flying, what a sight!
While ants in suits do take the stage,
In this wild, they're all the rage.

The trees are gossips, roots entwined,
Sharing secrets, oh so unrefined.
In bushes feasts and pranks unfold,
Nature's folly, so bold yet controlled.

Whispers of the Wild

A frog croaks out a love song loud,
With crickets forming quite the crowd.
The fireflies blink, a disco show,
While raccoons sneer, 'What a low blow!'

The snakes slide by, in stylish flair,
Wearing sunglasses, beyond compare.
They slither smooth, no care in sight,
In their world, it's all pure delight.

An owl hoots with a wise old grin,
While mice create a ruckus within.
Laughter echoes in leafy halls,
In nature's party, everyone balls.

Beneath the moon, the wild's a stage,
With giggles, dances, and no age.
In shadows deep, the fun won't cease,
In this realm, they find such peace.

The Uncharted Depths of Greenery

In tangled vines, a sloth takes pride,
Dreaming of snacks it'll never ride.
While ants march in a marching band,
They practice hard, by leaf they stand.

A turtle sings, but slow as can be,
Outpacing a snail—such majesty!
With a wink and nod, he shuffles past,
In this haste, fun's never cast.

The dandelions have a runway show,
With winds swirling, making seeds go.
They puff and fluff in sunset's light,
While shadows giggle, taking flight.

In the depths where laughter thrives,
Such odd friendships, oh how it drives.
In this green maze, both wild and free,
The tales unfold in pure glee.

A Tapestry of Shadowed Life

In the shades where the critters play,
A raccoon bakes with leaves in a tray.
Cooking up snacks from champignon,
While squirrels giggle, 'Is this a con?'

A beetle struts in shiny attire,
With dance moves that seem to inspire.
He spins and twirls in a dandy way,
Making the grasshopper shout, 'Booyay!'

A butterfly holds a beauty quiz,
While bugs debate, a grande fizz.
With buzzing friends wrapped in delight,
The shadows play till it's out of sight.

Each nook and cranny has tales to share,
Of critters wild, without a care.
In this wild maze, they paint their art,
A tapestry woven not far apart.

Cradle of the Wildflowers

In the meadow, blooms collide,
Bees buzzing, won't be denied.
Daisies dance with the wind's fun,
Sunlight whispers, 'Let's run!'

Petunias giggle, tulips tease,
Swaying gently with the breeze.
A butterfly, in silly flight,
Spills pollen with delight.

Birds in hats atop the boughs,
Chirp out loud their silly vows.
A dandelion's fluff spree,
Wishes blown, oh so carefree.

As evening drapes in twilight glow,
The flowers yawn, the laughter flows.
Under stars, the fun stays bright,
In the cradle of soft moonlight.

Beneath Billowing Clouds

Clouds like cotton, float on high,
Puffing out a friendly sigh.
Squirrels giggle in their fray,
Chasing shadows, come what may.

Raindrops tap a merry tune,
Making puddles, oh so soon.
Frogs in coats keep a fine beat,
Jumping joyfully on their feet.

Above, a stork in mismatched shoes,
Stumbles twice, then finds his muse.
A thunder clap, a rumble low,
Says, 'Don't fret! Just take it slow!'

Beneath this sky, a dance we weave,
Of light and laughter, just believe.
Each drip, each drop, a jovial shroud,
We find our fun beneath the cloud.

The Subterranean Ballad

Down below, the moles convene,
Fashion shows in dirt, so keen.
With tiny hats and burrowed pride,
They strut and stomp, a goofy ride.

Worms are critiquing the latest trends,
While mushrooms cheer, their little friends.
A party forms in tunnels tight,
With a glowworm DJ, spin it right!

Crickets play an underground song,
To which all critters dance along.
A party line of ants so spry,
With tiny moves, beneath the sky.

The echoes of their laughter swell,
In earthy chambers, all is well.
Under the ground, the fun abounds,
In secret realms, joy resounds!

Flutters in the Ferns

Ferns like dancers in a daze,
Waving lightly in a haze.
A critter hops from leaf to leaf,
Playing tag, a cheeky thief.

Butterflies clumsy on a breeze,
Flap and flutter, seek to please.
Their colors clash in vibrant hue,
Like a silly circus, it's true!

A rabbit with a wicked grin,
Joins the show, can't help but spin.
He tumbles down, but gets right back,
Wink at ferns, set on his track.

In the shade, the giggles rise,
As sunlight winks from the skies.
Here in this green, the laughter churns,
With every jiggle, joy returns!

Shadows Beneath Canopies

Beneath the trees, a squirrel pranced,
With acorns stolen, he happily danced.
A chipmunk chuckled, oh what a sight,
While frogs croaked jokes till the fall of night.

The owl gave a hoot, not a clue did he share,
As rabbits played tag without a care.
With mushrooms wearing tiny hats so neat,
All woodland folks joined in for a treat.

A beetle claimed he was quite the ace,
Rolling a leaf in his tiny space.
The forest floor echoed with giggles and glee,
As shadows waltzed in their leafy marquee.

So next time you wander where tree trunks weave,
Just look a bit closer, you might just believe.
For under the canopies, laughter is found,
In the silly antics of the critters around.

Whispers of the Woodland

In the glade, a whisper floats,
A rabbit in glasses reads forest notes.
The bear wears a scarf, oh what a flair,
While butterflies giggle without a care.

A hedgehog in boots taps a funny beat,
As ants make a line for a crumbly treat.
The trees tell secrets that giggle and sway,
In this merry woodland, come laugh and play.

The bees all buzz, sharing tales of the day,
Of flowers and sunbeams, and games they play.
Each rustle and chuckle breaks through the bark,
As critters convene for a lark in the park.

So if you should find, in the woods, a delight,
Listen close to the whispers that dance in the light.
For the woodland is filled with humor and cheer,
And the echoes of laughter are always quite near.

Secrets of the Lost Leaves

Beneath the oaks, secrets lie low,
Where leaves tell tales in the soft, breezy flow.
A squirrel with shades spins stories of nuts,
While the wise old toad keeps track of the cuts.

The crunch of the leaves brings giggles at best,
As raccoons in masks zip off for a fest.
With each little twirl and each rustle around,
The lost leaves reveal what laughter has found.

The underbrush sighs with chuckles and glee,
While a shy fox peeks from behind a tree.
The foliage whispers in a ticklish tone,
As critters conspire to play on their own.

With secrets that bubble and swell in the air,
Join in the fun if you haven't a care.
For the laughter of leaves is the best melody,
And the forest, a stage for a grand comedy.

Tales from the Forest Floor

On the forest floor, mischief does reign,
With mushrooms debating whose cap has the most gain.
A tortoise with style, he sports a sleek shell,
While crickets compose a sweet, chirpy swell.

Pinecones get serious, discussing their weight,
While ants hold a meeting to plan out their fate.
The grasshoppers leap with a bounce and a hop,
As laughter erupts, they just can't stop.

The fox in a hat, quite unusually grand,
Tells the best jokes which are truly unplanned.
The snickers and snorts echo low and near,
As pine needles dance to the forest's bright cheer.

So traipse through the woods, where the fun's in store,
In the tales of the forest, there's laughter galore.
For beneath every tree, in the cool shaded part,
Lie stories of joy that are sure to warm the heart.

The Hidden Symphony of Shade

In the grove where giggles sway,
Frogs complain about their day.
Squirrels dance with quite a flair,
While crickets tune their evening air.

Leaves are clapping, join the fun,
Mice are practicing their run.
A woodpecker beats time with grace,
As ants perform a classic race.

Every branch holds a secret note,
As owls watch from their comfy coat.
Trees hum softly, don't you hear?
Nature's tunes are oh-so-clear!

So come now, take a seat, my friend,
Join the show that will not end.
In this shady concert hall,
The laughter and the music call!

Where Shadows Bloom

In corners dark where mischief lurks,
Bunnies giggle and do their quirks.
The shadows bloom with silly sights,
As raccoons plan their midnight flights.

A turtle's slow but oh-so-slick,
Makes clownfish laugh with every trick.
While chipmunks try their best to glide,
But tumble down with joyful pride.

The flowers laugh, their petals wide,
They imagine what the ants might hide.
With whispers sweet like candy floss,
The shadows bloom, no time for loss!

It's a playground, wild and free,
With squirrels giggling in a tree.
So step right in, join the fun,
Where laughter blooms and shadows run!

Unseen Paths of Green

Through the ferns where no one peeks,
Lies a tale of grasshopper leaps.
A snail's race is quite absurd,
As hedgehogs cheer, 'You're the best, dear!'

Vines twist like they're in a dance,
While mushrooms play a game of chance.
The winding trails hide all the schemes,
Where every critter shares their dreams.

Ferny paths go round and round,
Bouncing laughter is the sound.
It seems the leaves are up to jest,
While bees debate who's dressed the best.

So take a step on this green track,
Where jokes are traded, never lack.
In unseen ways, life's full of cheer,
As laughter grows from ear to ear!

Chronicles of the Forest Depths

In the depths where mossy secrets lie,
Lop-eared bunnies ask 'Oh why?'
Why do the rocks giggle and sway?
They ponder while the frogs just play.

The snorts of boars blend with rhymes,
Painting stories through the times.
Owls croon softly, wise and old,
While snails tell tales, both brave and bold.

Dancing shadows cross the path,
Sprinkling smiles and gentle laughs.
If you peek close, you might find fun,
A world alive, second to none!

So wander deep with a light heart,
Join the forest to make your start.
With rhymes and giggles as your map,
You'll be surprised, life's a playful rap!

The Silent Display

In the woods where whispers play,
The mushrooms dance, they sway.
Frogs croak out their silly tunes,
While crickets wear their tiny loons.

Squirrels gossip with such flair,
Their acorns tossed with little care.
A raccoon joins the merry band,
And steals their snacks with sleight of hand.

The trees provide a shady stage,
While fireflies light up the page.
Even owls can't help but chuckle,
In this forest filled with shuffle.

So come along and join the spree,
Nature's jesters, wild and free.
With every rustle, giggle, and play,
Come revel in this bright ballet.

Kinship of the Undergrowth

Little critters hold a feast,
Ants march on, a merry beast.
The beetles brag and strut their stuff,
While slugs slide by, all soft and rough.

Beneath the ferns, they nod and wink,
Over shared snacks, they laugh and think.
A massive root becomes their throne,
As stories spin of seeds they've sown.

A squirrel juggles nuts with glee,
A turtle beats the drum with a tree.
Their kinship forms through silly pranks,
In this merry band, no one thanks.

They vow that laughter fills the air,
And friendship thrives with pelts to share.
In this lush land of leafy glee,
A family formed, forever free.

Stories from the Darkened Dell

In a dell where shadows creep,
A fox spins tales before sleep.
With glimmering eyes and a playful grin,
He tells of mischief, where to begin?

A badger chuckles from a mound,
While a hare bops around in circles, profound.
At nightfall, laughter fills the air,
When creatures gather, stories to share.

Mice with dreams of cheese-filled sails,
Raccoons boast of daring trails.
And while the night grows dark and deep,
Their giggles echo, no time for sleep.

So listen close and hear them tell,
Of brave adventures and wild spells.
In the dark, let joy be found,
With tales of fun constantly around.

Where Shadows Intertwine

In the dusk where shadows twine,
A chipmunk laughs at the moon's design.
Twirling leaves in mischief's game,
Each small critter seeks to gain fame.

A lizard slips through knotty vines,
While spiders weave their silly lines.
They gather round the glowing light,
For puns and pranks into the night.

A party forms without a care,
Each creature brought a game to share.
The playful tug of leafy tricks,
As friendships bloom in all the mix.

So, if you walk where shadows tease,
Join the choir of rustling leaves.
In this twilight, funny tales unfold,
A secret world of joy, behold!

Fables of the Rooted Family

In the shade a squirrel dreams,
Of acorns piled up like schemes.
He plots a route to gather more,
But forgets the stash right near his door.

The raccoons have a party plan,
With masks and dance, oh what a clan!
They swipe some snacks from right next door,
And leave the place a messy floor.

Old owl hoots a joke so dry,
It cracks the trees, oh my, oh my!
While rabbits giggle, tails a-fluff,
They can't stop laughing, it's too tough!

A hedgehog hosts a hair-styling night,
With prickly styles that cause delight.
They fashion 'dos with leaves and twine,
The trendsetters of the woodland line.

Veiled Tales from the Arboreal

Beneath the boughs, a tale unfolds,
Of critters wise, and antics bold.
The beaver's plans go all awry,
He built a dam, but missed the why.

A tale of branches, twigs, and fun,
Where squirrels race 'neath the setting sun.
With nutty bets and silly pranks,
They giggle and teeter on rickety planks.

The fox, he sings at moonlit nights,
Of lost socks and playful fights.
With each note, the woods awake,
And loudly they all dance and shake.

In hidden glades, a mystery brews,
Unseen creatures with fanciful views.
They whisper secrets of trees and dew,
Sharing giggles 'til the dawn breaks through.

Fragments of the Forest's Breathe

A wobbly deer trips over roots,
With flailing legs in mismatched boots.
She laughs it off and strikes a pose,
As nearby toads cheer on her toes.

The mushrooms hold a fencing match,
With tiny swords, they're hard to catch.
Their witty banter fills the air,
As frogs sit by without a care.

The clouds parade above so grand,
While trees dance lightly, hand in hand.
They twirl and whirl, in leafy threads,
While critters giggle in their beds.

A snarky crow starts an argument,
With wise old owls that won't relent.
Each caw and coo a comic feat,
As laughter ripples through the street.

Whispered Hues in the Shade

In the twilight, colors fade,
As fireflies start their masquerade.
The beetles show off their shiny backs,
While ladybugs trace tiny tracks.

The brook hums songs so sweet and clear,
While turtles gather near to cheer.
In waterlogged hats, they float and spin,
With ripples of laughter, they begin.

A roaming cat with a quirky strut,
Sneaks up on birds and mutters, 'What?'
But the birds just laugh and take to the sky,
While the cat sits down, wishing to fly.

At dusk, the woods wear a playful grin,
As shadows stretch and laughter wins.
Every leaf whispers jokes untold,
In the humor of nature, pure and bold.

The Layered Silence

In shadows deep, where whispers dwell,
A squirrel juggles acorns, oh what the hell!
Mice hold their meetings, plotting at night,
While owls roll their eyes, it's quite a sight!

With laughter muffled beneath the leaves,
A hedgehog plays poker, who believes?
The rabbit swaps tales of daring escapes,
As frogs croak along with their funny shapes.

Beneath the ferns, a dance-off commences,
The badger shows moves, that cure all expenses!
The laughter ripples through mossy high ground,
In this layered silence, joy is profound.

But shh, don't disturb this whimsical show,
For every chuckle, an echo will grow!
A giggle can reach the stars up above,
In the layered silence, we find all we love.

Journeys in the Gloom

In the gloom where mischief likes to nest,
A raccoon sets off on a treasure quest.
He snags a lost boot, oh what a find!
Squeezed in the left, the right is maligned!

Through tangled vines, he prances around,
With a clumsy charm that knows no bound.
The mushrooms giggle with each step he takes,
When he trips on a root that a tree snake makes.

In whispers of shadows, an echo chimes,
With frogs in tuxedos, they're short on rhymes.
Their banquet of flies served on crystal plates,
Makes for a feast that truly awaits!

With a wink and a flair, the critters take heed,
Of journeys in gloom, where laughter's the seed.
For even in dark, with mischief unfurled,
Are soirées of joy in this enchanted world.

Fables of the Forgotten Grove

In the grove where the wild tales grow,
A tortoise wears boots, stealing the show.
He wobbles along with a grand little strut,
While nearby a hedgehog gets stuck in a rut!

A canary croons songs of great might,
While the bees try to dance but just take flight.
They buzz and they whirl, in an awkward parade,
Claiming their throne as the "Queens of the Glade."

Fables of laughter, of pranks gone too far,
A fox with a hat claims he's now a czar!
The mushrooms roll eyes; they've seen it before,
As the critters join in with a raucous uproar.

With whispers of nonsense, and giggles on leaves,
The stories unfold as that sly fox deceives.
In the forgotten grove where all joys collide,
The fables of laughter are born side by side.

The Enchanted Earth

In the rustling grass, where secrets align,
A chipmunk makes pickles, oh isn't that fine?
With jars full of dreams, he offers a taste,
While ants hold a party, with nary a haste!

Beneath the tall trees, where shadows grow wide,
A snail hitches rides on a turtle's glide.
They laugh at the rush, as they stroll with such grace,
In a world where time slows, they find their sweet pace.

A dance of the daisies, they twist and they twirl,
While fireflies beam like the stars, in a whirl.
The enchanting hum of nature's great song,
Brings joy to the earth, where all fun belongs.

So join in the frolic, shed sorrows and fears,
For laughter ignites through the passing of years.
In the enchanted earth, where magic abounds,
Every chuckle and cheer, in our hearts it resounds.

Under the Veil of Starlit Leaves

In the moonlit night, squirrels conspire,
Planning mischief as leaves catch fire.
A raccoon dances, quite out of place,
Wearing a mask with a silly face.

Crickets chirp their applause in tune,
While fireflies glow like tiny balloons.
A hedgehog winks as he rolls on by,
'This party's wild!' he says with a sigh.

Branches sway, whispering secrets bold,
Of toadstool tea parties, tales untold.
'Owl,' says the fox, 'you look quite dapper!'
'I'm just here for snacks,' came the wise old crapper.

The night wears on, laughter fills the air,
All critters gather, with naught a care.
Under starlit leaves, joy's the decree,
Who knew forest life could be so free?

The Quiet Chronicles of the Green

Beneath the ferns, a rooster's dispute,
With a sleepy owl in winged pursuit.
'You're too noisy!' the owl hoots in fright,
'It's way too early! Just take flight!'

A snail, wearing shades, slicks back his shell,
'This groove is mine; I'm under a spell!'
A rabbit jumps in, all floppy and spry,
'Chill out, dude,' with a wink and a sigh.

The mushrooms gossip in colors so bright,
'Who wore that coat? Oh, what a fright!'
While ladybugs gossip in polka dot hues,
About the latest blooms and garden ruse.

Yet amidst the silence, a tumbleweed rolls,
In a twist of fate, gaining new goals.
Nature's antics create quite the scene,
Laughter echoing through the shades of green.

Reverberations in the Shadowed Realm

Beneath the canopy of a tangled mess,
A chubby squirrel has lost his dress.
He's searching the branches, in quite a fix,
All while singing some silly six-pick.

An ant parade marches with pomp and pride,
Carrying crumbs on a troublesome ride.
A wise old turtle, slow on his way,
Just rolls his eyes at the youthful display.

The shadows laugh, sharing tales of the night,
Of a cricket's waltz and an owl's delight.
With glowworms glowing, like stars all around,
Even the trees join the laughter profound.

In the midst of all, a shadow takes flight,
A bat with sunglasses, oh what a sight!
'You humans sleep while we have our fun,
Under the moon, we're wild and we run!'

Harmony of the Leafy Refuge

In a leafy nook where laughter thrives,
A family of badgers shares crazy dives.
'Who took the last berry?' cries out the kid,
While mum rolls her eyes, and the dad just hid.

A gopher emerges with a grand old tale,
Of his tunnel adventures and a forgotten snail.
Worms wiggle and squirm with stories to share,
Of the wild raccoon and his flamboyant hair.

The leaves rustle softly, a giggly breeze,
As a bunch of frogs throw a splashy tease.
'Come join the fun!' croaks the oldest of all,
And suddenly, splashes ring through the hall.

In harmony here, amidst smiles so bright,
The leafy refuge holds wonders each night.
With giggles and joy, under branches so wide,
Life's playful cadence brings nature's pride.

Hidden Lives of the Woodlands

Squirrels gossip in tree top chats,
While raccoons argue over their hats.
A fox with style prances along,
Whistling tunes to a skipping song.

Mice throw parties after the rain,
Baking thimbleberry pie with no grain.
A hedgehog DJ spins records loud,
While owls hoot, forming a crowd.

Worms in the dirt throw a wild feast,
Complaining about their life as a beast.
Beetles roll dice, fate on a line,
While ants march smart, their plans to define.

The woods are alive with laughter and cheer,
Mysteries unfold that are far from mere.
Nature's jesters play tricks every day,
In the hidden lives where the odd things play.

Beneath the Boughs of Time

The toad sings ballads, croaks in delight,
Chasing shadows that dart in the night.
A turtle spins tales, slow as a rhyme,
Adventuring close to the barriers of time.

Crickets dream loudly, in rhythmic tune,
Plotting grand heists to steal the moon.
A wise old owl gives advice from the air,
While bats in capes toss and turn without care.

Woodpeckers knock for a doorbell surprise,
Raccoons peek out with mischievous eyes.
The dance of the leaves holds secrets so vast,
With each tiny rustle a giggle from the past.

Funny whispers drift through the glade,
Where every creature in fervor parades.
Such a peculiar place, you might find,
A universe playing games with your mind.

Between the Roots and Dreams

In the realm where mushrooms sprout,
Frogs leap high with a joyful shout.
A dragonfly winks as it skitters by,
Chasing clouds in a breezy sky.

Ants build castles, quite proud of their quest,
While spiders weave tapestries with zest.
"Come join our feast!" the fireflies plea,
As they sprinkle glow like confetti tree.

The raccoons declare themselves nobles of night,
Dancing on rocks, feeling just right.
While a snoring bear snoozes near by,
Dreaming of honey and a big pie.

In this world beneath roots so deep,
Where silliness lurks and shadows leap.
Life is a laugh, not a serious scheme,
Just a silly place of whimsy and dream.

Stories from the Shaded Realm

Bunnies gossip over grass so lush,
Comparing hats in a pre-spring rush.
A lizard jogs, looking slick and spry,
With sunglasses on, waving goodbye.

The river sings tunes that swirl and blend,
Where fish in tuxedos swim, just pretend.
A clam claps loud, a shellfish applause,
As ducks in a line strut without flaws.

In the slow dance of shadows and light,
A chameleon plays tricks through the night.
Gathering tales that tickle and tease,
In a realm where laughter flows with ease.

Oh, the tales they tell beneath leafy shields,
Where fantasy thrives and magic yields.
This shaded realm sings with giggles galore,
And hints of mischief forever in store.

The Enigma of the Darkened Earth

In shadowy depths where secrets creep,
The critters gather for a giggly sweep.
A raccoon juggles acorns with flair,
While squirrels plot mischief sans a care.

Beneath the ferns, a snail does race,
With a feathered hat and a smirking face.
The groundhog bets it can dig a hole,
But trips on roots and loses control.

A mole composes tunes in the dirt,
A symphony made of old t-shirts.
Earthworms dance, they wiggle and sway,
With wormy friends in a cabaret.

But caution, my friend, as laughter grows,
For the giggling mushrooms have pinky toes.
They tickle the toes of those who dare,
In this darkened earth, fun's everywhere!

Beneath the Sunlit Trellis

Beneath the sun's warm, golden glow,
A beetle boasts of his famous show.
He twirls and spins, a dazzling sight,
As ladybugs applaud with delight.

The vines are gossiping, oh what fun,
About the fly who thinks he can run.
He trips on petals, lands with a thud,
And giggles echo through the garden mud.

A bumblebee hums a silly tune,
While dancing with blooms 'neath the lazy moon.
Forget-me-nots chuckle at grasshopper quips,
As butterflies swoon, doing backflips.

But watch your step in this playful scene,
For frogs juggle insects like rubber beans.
In a world where laughter takes center stage,
The sunlit trellis is a comic page!

Flora and Fauna Fables

The flowers tell tales of the bees they know,
Who steal sweet nectar with a classy bow.
A dandelion dreams of being a star,
But she floats away on a breeze from afar.

A wise old owl hoots with jolly glee,
Sharing secrets to squirrels stuck up a tree.
His tales of adventure are quite a delight,
As acorns rumble in a curious fight.

The hedgehog finds fortune in piles of leaves,
Trading sharp quills for shiny achievements.
A garden party with bugs plays their song,
All singing together, right where they belong.

But keep an ear tuned for the crafty crow,
Who steers the gossip, putting on quite a show.
In flora and fauna, the fun never ends,
As each little creature is more than a friend!

Whimsy in the Wilderness

In the wilderness where the wild things play,
A fox with a top hat saunters away.
He tips it with style, strutting his stuff,
While giggling rabbits declare it's enough!

A pair of raccoons in a puppet show,
With acorns and twigs, they put on a glow.
The audience cheers, it's a raucous cheer,
As the woodland critters all draw near.

A deer in a tutu prances about,
With daisies and dandelions, there's no doubt.
Her pirouettes send the frogs into fits,
While turtles bicker over perfect splits.

But watch for the bear, he's plotting a prank,
With honey and jam, he'll leave his tank.
In whimsy and laughter, the woods come alive,
Where every creature knows how to thrive!

The Secret Heart of the Glade

In a glade where gnomes dance with flair,
Mushrooms giggle in sunlight's glare.
Frogs wear crowns, oh what a sight,
They croak of kings on this fine night.

Squirrels argue over acorn stashes,
While rabbits race in silly crashes.
The wise old owl just shakes his head,
He's too busy counting his bread.

Bees are buzzing a tune so sweet,
While spiders twirl on silken feet.
Each leaf holds secrets, oh so grand,
Of a world that's just slightly unplanned.

So if you wander, take a peek,
At the laughter where nature speaks.
For in every nook there's a tale to spin,
With critters laughing, let the fun begin!

Tales from the Shadows

In shadows deep where whispers roam,
A raccoon plots to steal your comb.
He moonlights as a style guru,
With fashion tips for squirrels too.

The hedgehog dreams of being bold,
Wearing spikes but wishes for gold.
He carries a purse, oh what a sight,
Collecting trinkets late at night.

A fox writes sonnets under a tree,
About the winds and the bumblebee.
His rhymes are funny, a real delight,
He ruffles feathers and takes flight!

So tiptoe softly and keep it low,
In these shadows, the pranks will flow.
For every nook has laughter tucked,
In the tales of creatures, happily mucked.

Echoes of the Subtle Canopy

Beneath the leaves where whispers thrive,
A bird mocks a goat, oh what a jive!
They swap funny stories of nimble feet,
And how they both avoid a beet.

The trees gossip in rustling tones,
About the squirrels making their homes.
Filling their pockets with acorns galore,
While the porcupine waits by the door.

Whimsical shadows dance in the sun,
As beetles race just for fun.
With laughter echoing through the boughs,
Nature chuckles and humbly bows.

So take a moment and tune your ear,
To giggles and chatter that linger near.
For in the subtle spaces we find,
Echoes of joy to expand the mind.

What Lies Beneath the Green

Beneath the green where mushrooms play,
A family of ants dance every day.
They have a party with tiny treats,
While snails serve punch on their little feats.

The grasshoppers host a wild jam,
With crickets singing, oh who's the sham?
Jaybirds show up, flaunting their wings,
Claiming they're royalty while everyone sings.

A hedgehog juggles with berries and leaves,
While ladybugs plot with webs up their sleeves.
In tunnels below, mischief is rife,
They laugh and play in this funny life.

So peek through the blades and take a look,
At a world where giggles and gigabytes cook.
For what lies beneath is a laugh galore,
In this tangled green, there's so much more!

Life in the Leaf Litter

In the damp and messy ground,
Squirrels toss acorns all around.
A worm with dreams of grand ballet,
Sings loudly, but no one's in the fray.

Beneath the rotting leaves, they play,
A colony of ants led astray.
They march with snacks upon their backs,
But one forgot his lunch—oh, what a crack!

A slug slides by with steady grace,
While toads discuss their nightly race.
A tiny frog hops, thinks he's a king,
Sings of marshmallows, on a string.

So here beneath the mossy shroud,
Nature's misfits—oh, they're so loud!
Each critter with their silly plot,
A comedy show that hits the spot!

Murmurs of the Hidden Grove

In shadows where the gossip brews,
Trees whisper tales of old-world blues.
A rabbit shares a joke on the moose,
While bees buzz in a sarcastic truce.

Beneath the boughs, the mushrooms leer,
"Oh, how we make the deer appear!"
A squirrel with acorns in his cheeks,
Pretends to be wise, but oh, how he squeaks!

The crow croaks out a witty jest,
As butterflies flutter in a pastel vest.
Together they chuckle at the sun's glare,
"Why did the leaf get caught in the hair?"

In the grove, where secrets collide,
Each creature's charm cannot hide.
So listen close, and you may find,
A nutty world that's one of a kind!

Dances of the Silent Foliage

Dancing leaves on a breezy day,
Twirl and flutter, come what may.
A gopher's groove on the forest floor,
Reveals he's got moves we can't ignore.

A family of mushrooms takes the lead,
In polka dots, they dance with speed.
Even the shadows sway with delight,
While crickets chirp into the night.

The owl hoots out a steady beat,
While fireflies flash their glowing feet.
Raccoons join in, with a little clap,
Caught in the joy, they take a nap.

In this quiet party, without sound,
Nature's rhythm spins us round.
So shake your leaves, don't be shy,
Join the jest, let laughter fly!

Colors of the Forest Underbelly

In hues of brown and softest green,
A painter's palette, so serene.
But wait, what's this? A patch so bright,
A mushroom that glows like disco night!

There's a cactus that thinks he's the star,
With prickly fluff and much too far.
While chipmunks strut in flashy coats,
Debating who has the best anecdotes.

A log calls out, "Hey, look at me!
I'm a bridge for bugs, don't you see?"
And nearby, snails in a race so slow,
Declare the winner, but nobody knows!

For down in the depths where laughter lies,
Life blooms brightly behind the guise.
In every shade and silly tale,
The forest giggles, we cannot fail!

www.ingramcontent.com/pod-product-compliance
Lightning Source LLC
Chambersburg PA
CBHW072137200426
43209CB00050B/112